IMAGES
of America

FAIR HAVEN

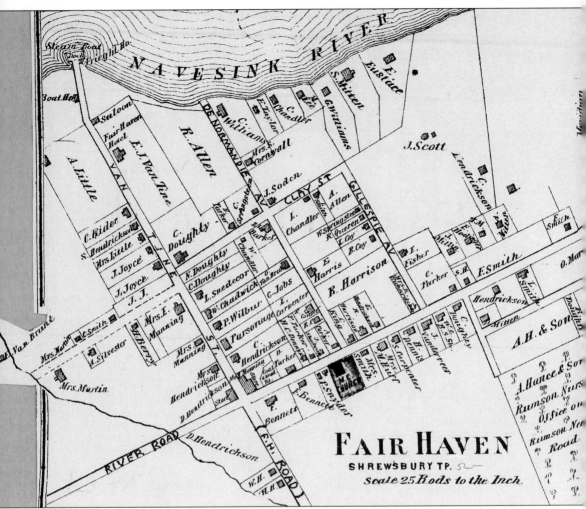

The village plan from Plate 35 of the 1873 *Beers, Comstock and Cline Atlas of Monmouth County* shows a growing town about a quarter-century after the erection of a dock solidified Fair Haven's grip on maritime life. The town, then a neighborhood of Shrewsbury Township, appears to have developed from its eastern stem at the right of the map, westward. The J. Scott (p. 30) and F. Smith (not illustrated) houses are among Fair Haven's existing oldest. The earliest, Jeremiah Chandler's, has been reported as having been on either of two plots, requiring further investigation. The borough's historic district is centered around the streets named in the plan above. Most of its early structures still stand. The property owners on this map reflect a "who's who" of early Fair Haven. Their names also appear regularly in the captions.

IMAGES
of America

FAIR HAVEN

Randall Gabrielan

ARCADIA

First published 1997
Copyright © Randall Gabrielan, 1997

ISBN 0-7524-0434-2

Published by Arcadia Publishing,
an imprint of the Chalford Publishing Corporation,
One Washington Center, Dover, New Hampshire 03820.
Printed in Great Britain

Library of Congress Cataloging-in-Publication Data applied for

This book is dedicated to the Honorable Theodore J. Labrecque, one of Monmouth County's most esteemed citizens, and a former resident of Fair Haven who still practices law here in his tenth decade. Even if one overlooked his public and personal accomplishments —they would fill this page—Judge Labrecque deserves honor and respect for his enthusiastic support of his fellow historians, support backed with a generosity of spirit and materials that makes a fine model to emulate. That generosity has helped imbue this historian with his own ethic of helping others.

Contents

Acknowledgments

The springboard for this project was the fine family collection of Marilyn Willis, who generously shared her images and provided cheerful, enthusiastic encouragement from the outset. She receives my greatest and heartfelt thanks. Most of her pictures were photographed by her great-grandfather, Christopher Doughty Chandler. He did not intend to provide the foundation for a book, but by recording glimpses of his town's history he unwittingly did just that. Few towns are fortunate enough to have such a vivid pictorial record from their early years. Fewer authors are privileged to have such liberal access to it. Fair Haven and I are, indeed, fortunate for his pioneering work.

Fair Haven resident John Rhody contributes regularly to the author's publications. His major impact on this volume entitles him to take significant pride at seeing his hometown in print. Thanks, once more, John.

Special thanks to Karen L. Schnitzspahn for her theatrical images, including the one featured on the cover. Historian Karen, lending from the core of her specialty, shows a high degree of generosity, concern, and interest in my work, and receives my deepest thanks and appreciation.

Photography Unlimited by Dorn's is building its Fair Haven archives in a manner that will allow the collection to have a major impact on the borough's historic imagery. My thanks to them for being part of the preservation process.

Danny Sanchez is an exceptionally talented portrait photographer with an uncanny ability to reveal character and personality in his subjects. It is a pleasure to publish one of his portraits.

George Fox is a photographer's photographer whose love for the art turns out superlative work, whether from behind the lens or in the darkroom. He printed several Christopher Chandler glass plates, most untouched for over three-quarters of a century, a helpful gesture that enhanced the quality of the book.

The new Historical Association of Fair Haven, although without a collection, has spearheaded a renaissance of interest in Fair Haven's history. Their efforts contribute to a favorable environment for this publication and merit my recognition and thanks.

Thanks also to the lenders of the photographs, whether of one or many, who are the co-producers of this volume. An extra measure of appreciation goes to those who took the initiative to seek me out to offer their material. They are Harold Albert; Candy and Ray Bennett; Olga Boeckel; Lois Bodtmann; Ed Brett; Bobbi Campbell; Diane Carmona; Richard Cheu, skipper of the River Rats; Kenneth Curchin; Susan Donaldson; Richard F. Doughty; Patricia Ann Drummond; Joseph Eid; Robert B. Ender; Carolyn L. Feist; Gail Hunton; Bernard Kellenyi; David Kennedy; the Honorable Theodore J. Labrecque; John Lentz; Scott Longfield; Joan Lucky; Patrick S. Mason; the Monmouth County Historical Association; Ralph Mulford Jr.; Lucy Nickerson; Virginia Smith Paine; Helen Pike (for reference material); Margaret Post; Joan Rice; Newton Rice Jr.; Joseph Robertson; Rutgers University Libraries, Special Collections and Archives; Lynda and Thomas Santry Jr.; Sandi von Pier; and last, but he is used to it, Robert Zerr.

Introduction

Fair Haven was initially part of the vast expanse of sparsely settled land that comprised Shrewsbury Township, one of Monmouth County's three original townships. Property in the future Fair Haven was narrowly held into the second quarter of the nineteenth century, much of it owned by the DeHart family, who acquired it from Mauritz DeHaert's 1762 purchase of 181 acres on the Navesink River from Francis Borden. Reports have circulated that the area was called DeHartsville, but the author has never seen contemporary accounts or older maps indicating that name.

The river shore was likely long worked and lived upon by a handful of pioneers. Historically, the area was also home to a number of free African-Americans. Jacob Brown bought property in 1830 around Browns Lane, although his family claimed Browns were here much earlier. The town appears to have developed from east to west.

Instances of settlement before the middle of the eighteenth century include the construction of the Scott house (p. 30), the establishment of the A.M.E. Zion Church in 1833, the formation of a school district in 1841, the organization of the Methodists by 1843, the beginning of John Covert's store in 1825, and the building of Jeremiah Chandler's house in 1816.

Fair Haven's dock is believed to have been built prior to 1850, without evidence of its actual construction. Fair Haven is not named on the 1851 Lightfoot Monmouth County map, nor is it in Thomas F. Gordon's 1834 *Gazetteer of the State of New Jersey*. Growth in the 1850s was rapid; the town merited a village plan in the 1860 Beers map, perhaps the first publication of the name. The historic district was in place on the next Monmouth map, the 1873 *Beers, Comstock and Cline Atlas* (p. 2). The dock helped make Fair Haven Road the main north-south street in town.

Red Bank influenced western Fair Haven. Both towns were dotted with street-to-river estates. Fair Haven's first major development, East Side Park, was promoted as providing sites for new housing which were outside, but still close to, town. When Fair Haven sought to form a borough, Red Bank also desired East Side Park.

Henry Miner's attraction of an entertainment following also affected Fair Haven. The acting crowd recognized the "be oneself" quality of Fair Haven, a place with neither Red Bank's commercial intensity, nor Rumson's pretension. Rumson helped populate Fair Haven, a town where workers on Rumson estates could secure their own homes.

Fair Haven at the century's end was active and growing. Its waterfront and commercial stem thrived. Two churches were long established, its school was expanded twice, and meeting halls were built. A fire department was formed in 1904. Many thought home rule desirable. Both forming boroughs and annexation by adjoining municipalities were often easy under New Jersey law then. Fair Haven had considered incorporation at least since 1893, when large property owners opposed the plan. The issue was discussed for years and success was thought to have been obtained in 1911. However, some interests wished to retain Fair Haven in the township, and Red Bank desired the western part of the proposed borough, so independence was not obtained until 1912. It is thought that Thomas McCarter's opposition was a factor in the 1911 failure.

Fair Haven's suburbanization was typical. Transportation and commercial fishing declined on the river, but recreational use of the waterway increased. Open tracts sprouted housing. Strained schools were expanded. Changes in the locations and numbers of churches followed, including the addition of a Roman Catholic church and the relocation of the Methodist church, both in out-lying areas with parking.

The commercial mix changed, both in type and location of stores. The hotels are gone, along with their entertainment clientele. The actors' boat club long ago faced the reality of its dwindling numbers and "mainstreamed" its membership. However, the original appeal of Fair Haven remains. It is a place where one can be oneself, a town like neither of its neighbors, and a place where one feels part of a personal town, rather than an impersonal suburb. Fair Haven is not immune to change, which some old-timers claim is too prevalent; but while nothing remains static, Fair Haven has retained its sense of community, a caring populace, and a relaxed, warm atmosphere. The author hopes these qualities are conveyed herein.

Readers should note that picture availability and space determine what images are included in a work such as this. The author hopes that a future volume will remedy conspicuous absences and under-representation, particularly of the acting colony. If you can help with a second volume, please contact the author at 71 Fish Hawk Drive, Middletown, NJ 07748, or (908) 671-2645.

One
Maritime Activity

The building of a dock, probably in the 1840s, is likely the single event that transformed a handful of waterfront settlers into a community. Although many vessels stopped here, it is the *Albertina* that is most closely associated with Fair Haven. It is the craft on the borough's seal, which was introduced at the 1962 municipal golden jubilee. This photograph was taken by Christopher Chandler on August 31, 1908.

The Merchants Steamboat Company operated the *Albertina*, built as a 165-foot-long craft in 1882 and extended by 9 feet later in the 1880s. It plied the Navesink into the 1930s carrying, in addition to passengers and freight, horses, carriages, and moving vans of summer residents from the city. This image is from a *c.* 1910 postcard.

The *Sea Bird*, the longest running steamer on the New York-Navesink River route, is seen in a *c.* 1910 postcard. The run began in 1866, the year of the steamer's construction, and continued for sixty years. This 182-foot-long vessel was built by Edward Minturn, a New Yorker with a summer home on the Navesink at Rocky Point, and Moses Taylor, who had one of the most important Elberon, Long Branch, cottages. The *Sea Bird* sustained a serious fire in 1867, but returned to service the following year.

The steamer dock also provided an opportunity for recreation, as indicated by these youthful fishers on a *c.* 1910 postcard.

The steamboat dock is viewed looking west, showing its storage building. Also visible on this *c.* 1910 postcard is a glimpse of part of the Grand View Hotel, once located on the west side of the foot of Fair Haven Road.

This mud digger was employed as part of a spring 1910 attempt to deepen Fourth Creek. The Harvey M. Little Sr. house is visible at left and on p. 41.

Harvey M. Little, born in Fair Haven c. 1845, remained a lifelong resident and was active as a waterman. Little died in October 1915 after entering his boat off Island Beach in Sandy Hook, where he had been a member of a camping party for a week. He was survived by seven children.

The view of the mouth of Fourth Creek on p. 112 suggests it was once a navigable waterway. However, an absence of contemporary accounts leaves one wondering just what type of maritime activity the creek saw.

The two views of Fourth Creek, both *c.* 1909, suggest navigability by smaller craft of either fishing or recreational types.

Edward M. Little was born *c.* 1875 in Fair Haven, remaining a lifelong resident of the area. He spent about fifty years in boating, taking his first job at age fourteen with the Patten Line on the New York to Long Branch run, obtaining a pilot's license at age twenty-one. Little, seen here around 1915, married the former Clara Minton, and their union endured over fifty years. The couple lived at 703 River Road; he died in 1955.

Captain Edward M. Little, seen on an unidentified vessel around 1905, was first the captain of the *Sea Bird*. He captained that ship and the *Albertina* for thirty-two years. Captain Little had earlier served on the *Pleasure Bay*, the *Little Silver*, and *Oceanus*, and later in his career on the Hudson River excursion boat *Ossining*.

River Road is now the northernmost east-west thoroughfare on the Red Bank-Rumson peninsula. An earlier road along the waterway is described as a path along the river. This early-century view depicts a remnant of a road that by then had been replaced by today's route.

These two views show Clinton Wilber in his iceboat on February 25, 1912. Iceboats are classified in several categories by sail size. Robert D. Chandler, a noted Fair Haven architect, also built iceboats.

Wilber's boat is "lifting." Iceboats encounter little resistance on the ice and can travel "faster that the wind."

This image depicts Frank Bennett's iceboat on February 20, 1910. The boater sails in a lying-down position, creating an unusual feeling of closeness to the ice.

Four boaters prepare for the start of an "ice yacht" (an alternate term) race on January 8, 1910. Iceboat racing is still popular, although the river freezes less frequently than it did decades ago. The sport is headquartered in the area at the North Shrewsbury Ice Boat & Yacht Club in Red Bank, an organization founded in 1880.

W.N. Chandler and crew were photographed oystering on the Navesink on January 20, 1910, by Christopher Doughty Chandler. The *Register* of January 25, 1893, gave a guide to gathering oysters in the ice, a process often difficult and even dangerous. The usual plan is to cut a hole in the ice . . .

. . . 20 or 30 feet long and 6 or 7 feet wide. A plank is thrown across the opening, on which the oysterman stands raking up his oysters. On thick ice, it was often more work to cut the ice and keep the area clear of snow than it was to pick up the oysters.

Carmen Rice and guest Howard G. Strauss pause for the photographer in front of the Rice home. Straus was a Shrewsbury resident and businessman. His Broad Street estate, which now includes the site of the Monmouth County Eastern Branch Library, can be seen in Arcadia's *Shrewsbury* on pp. 60–61.

A variety of winter sports are portrayed in this Christopher Chandler photograph of Coverts Cove taken on February 22, 1908.

The Fair Haven shore attracted a large number of pleasure-seekers on August 11, 1940.

The Fair Haven Yacht Works is shown here in the 1920s. Earlier known as the Kotick Boat Works, named after its founder, the business was sold to William I. Buchanan in 1927.

Henry J. Miner, a major New York theater owner, vaudeville promoter, and manager of stars, owned a substantial estate on Fair Haven's western shore. He attracted a following, establishing a major entertainment presence in Fair Haven, one that continued and grew following his death in 1900. Miner and his associates chose a houseboat on the river as their social headquarters. This Charles Foxwell photograph shows the opening of the entertainers' first home on July 4, 1910.

The boat's modest $250 cost presented an obstacle to overcome. The members of the newly organized Players Boat Club applied their assets in an expected manner by putting on a show, traveling to Red Bank's Frick Lyceum in an open motorcade. The players' show became an annual event. This undated picture, perhaps c. 1930, is titled "The Cast Party." (Collection of Karen L. Schnitzspahn.)

The players' initial home was inadequate, which resulted in the purchase of a larger houseboat for $ 2,500. It was towed from Coney Island Creek, in Brooklyn, to Fair Haven, spending its first winter in Fourth Creek. This c. 1920s postcard is believed to depict the second home. (Collection of John Rhody.)

A new clubhouse was built in 1929, designed by Red Bank architect Ernest A. Arend to appear not unlike the traditional houseboat. It was erected 110 feet from the shore on pilings by S.S. Thompson & Co. of Red Bank, opening in July with a dance and cabaret that strained the structure's capacity. This image is from a c. 1940s postcard. (Collection of John Rhody.)

The club had a two-tiered membership, consisting of "lay" members (who had no voice in operations) and professionals. The group faced the reality of a dwindling number of actors, reorganizing itself in 1939 as the Shrewsbury River Yacht Club, reflecting the Navesink's longtime alternate name of the North Shrewsbury River. Change occurred after this 1950 photograph. Large picture windows separated by a door replaced the six original windows at left. A sun porch has been built on the north, or water, end. (Special Collections and Archives, Rutgers University Libraries.)

A large reception room dominated the clubhouse's first floor, surrounded on the exterior by a promenade. A kitchen and other club facilities were built on the second floor. This is a 1960s postcard view. (Collection of John Rhody.)

Henry G. Wickham, a Springfield, Ohio, native, owned and operated the Wickham Piano Plate Co., a business founded by his father. He bought the Fair Haven Yacht Works and the Toms River Boat Works in the early 1930s. During World War II, the piano business was used for the storage of war materials, while Wickham converted the Fair Haven operation to produce small craft for the military. (Collection Monmouth County Historical Association.)

The custom-built yacht operation was obviously suspended for the duration. It is gratifying to see a detail-oriented army date their pictures so effectively, eliminating the often-thorny process of estimated dating. (Collection Monmouth County Historical Association.)

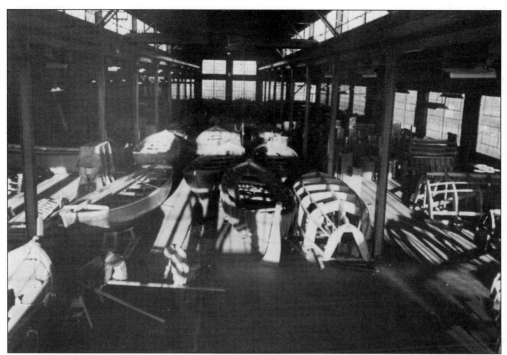

This interior shot of the Fair Haven Yacht Works was taken during the 1943 production of military craft. (Collection Monmouth County Historical Association.)

The Fair Haven Yacht Works twice received an Army-Navy "E" Award for excellence. Wickham is seen accepting the honors on March 19, 1943. He resumed piano production after the war. Wickham, a Middletown resident since about 1935, died in 1987 at age ninety-four. (Collection Monmouth County Historical Association.)

The worst fire in the borough's history destroyed the Fair Haven Yacht Works and about forty-five boats on December 15, 1965. The fire quickly engulfed the entire yard after apparently starting in a lumber storage area behind the office, causing a million-dollar loss. That was big money then. One injury was reported: a face burn. The premises were rebuilt and are in operation today at the foot of De Normandie Avenue. (The Dorn's Collection.)

Dads of Fair Haven, Inc., a group widely known as the River Rats, was formed in September 1954 to promote the maritime recreation and education of youth. The group built and sailed boats, teaching seamanship, primarily using the property of Walter Isbrandtsen, a noted shipping executive, lawyer, and licensed officer of the Merchant Marine. Isbrandtsen was the driving force of the organization in its formative years. He secured a lease for the landing at the foot of Battin Road; when the landing was lost in 1958, he responded by securing a floating home.

Isbrandtsen acquired the barge *Mona*, had it towed from New York Harbor, and anchored it about 300 feet off the Fair Haven public dock. The process had the approval of the borough's council and the New Jersey Bureau of Navigation, but prompted vigorous opposition from adjacent homeowners. The craft, converted for the club's use and christened the *Pied Piper* on August 2, 1959, had storage space for boats and recreational facilities. On October 7, 1959, it broke loose from its 4,000-pound mooring (despite a new anchor chain), drifted across the river, and ran aground on the Middletown shore.

Isbrandtsen, believing sabotage was the cause of the accident, moved the *Pied Piper* to winter storage as the state revoked its mooring permit. The craft was sold and converted to a restaurant on Staten Island. The River Rats returned to Battin Road, acquiring the property despite opposition by local property owners. The group established itself as a volunteer, non-profit educational organization, and continues to maintain boating programs. (With thanks to Richard A. Cheu, River Rats skipper, for the three photographs and background information.)

The usually placid Navesink River has its stormy spells and was rarely rougher than during the 1993 northeaster. The boat shown here, photographed from the shore at the west side of Fair Haven Road, was soon beached.

The Fair Haven dock is seen submerged during the 1993 northeaster. Newton Rice Jr. took the two photographs, while nephew Brian Rice held him to preclude his blowing away. Their death-defying efforts certainly merit a credit line.

Two

A Residential Borough

River Road is seen looking west near Sunset Terrace. The Christopher Doughty home is at number 882, adjacent to the telephone pole (which was eliminated on the printed postcard version of this image). Above Joseph Salz's sign ("For Bargains in Dry Goods") is the little-changed number 890. The stone fence marks Doughty Lane. The porch on number 868 at the eastern corner has been enclosed; number 876 is behind the fence. Number 852, the place with two chimneys and two attic windows, can now see the dawn's early light through a window added on the first floor's northeast corner. On the north side, a new house has been squeezed between number 895 (to the right) and number 867 (above it). George Fox printed Christopher Chandler's glass plate made on November 4, 1907.

James Scott began buying Fair Haven land in 1845. Brightwood Cottage was the later boarding-house name for the former Scott house at 48 Gillespie Avenue, seen here on a c. 1910 postcard. One of Fair Haven's oldest buildings, its varied history was described in a December 21, 1899 *Register* account that was written when the property was sold to Rufus Merritt. The property served for periods of time as a school and grocery store. The land, having a 504-foot frontage on the river, was divided, and several houses were built on it.

This c. 1900 view of the Brightwood Cottage appears to show the north, or river, facade. The expanse of lawn was greater than at present, but the house is still recognizable. However, a wing was added on the east and at least one chimney has been replaced. The house at left, part of the Brightwood property, has been replaced with an enormous new house.

This *c.* 1910 postcard view is identified as "Cove Near Brightwood Cottages," an area that was changed following its division after the 1899 purchase by Rufus Merritt and the erection of several houses.

William L. Hedenberg's 1903 house on the river at the foot of Gillespie Avenue was designed by the short-lived partnership of Chandler and Shoemaker. The house, bearing elements of Bungalow style, was likely the work of William A. Shoemaker, as it bears no stylistic resemblance to the known work of Robert D. Chandler, who was about to retire to build boats. Hedenberg sold it to Harry Angelo in 1914. The house was reported to have been expanded to two stories, still occupying its original site. Storms have destroyed the fine stone bulkhead.

The Fair Haven shore from the Shrewsbury River Yacht Club on the east (left) to the public dock on the west (right) is seen in a c. 1969 aerial by John Lentz. Browns Lane, the street above the club, was an early free African-American settlement, but its old fabric has been devastated by new construction in recent years. Fair Haven Road, a long north-south street, ends at the dock, beginning at Rumson Road in front of the Rumson Country Club golf course, which is

shown in the background. Clay Street is the two-block-long east-west street in the historic district, seen above the Fair Haven Yacht Works, which is at the foot of De Normandie Avenue. Gillespie Avenue is the district's other short north-south street. Note how this street, running to the river, contains waterfront property by virtue of its lot layout. McCarters Pond is the body of water in the middle of the picture.

Two trolleys are passing at the Gillespie Avenue switch while the photographer is looking east from near 800 River Road. That house had an octagonal tower added on the west and a wing on the east. The building's exterior is unchanged from this c. 1907 image, but the first floor is now studio and retail space, occupied by communication designers McCann-Cobran on the west and the collectors gallery "What A Doll" on the east.

Dr. George Van V. Warner is parked with his horse in front of his residence at 800 River Road in 1912. He was selected as the first borough physician that year. Dr. Warner, born in West Fulton, New York, graduated from New York Medical College in Albany. He was a trustee of the Hazard Hospital, Long Branch, and was a member (and later president) of the Monmouth County Mosquito Control Commission. Dr. Warner resided in Red Bank at his death in 1944.

The G.W. Smith residence at 834 River Road, shown here in 1911, was a Queen Anne-style house, built *c.* 1908. It is well preserved, with some changes built on its west.

The small house at 826 River Road, perhaps pre-dating 1850, is little changed since this *c.* 1880s photograph with unidentified occupants. The porch is now enclosed and a new roof has a lower pitch.

Kemp Avenue is seen looking south on August 16, 1911. Number 23 is at left, a house that appears to have been later raised to two and one half stories, with the porch enclosed. The Pine View Hotel is the other building, the two separated by Sycamore Lane.

The Pine View Hotel was designed by William A. Shoemaker of Red Bank and built for Emma G. Miller by Ira D. Emery in the summer of 1910. It is now a private residence, little changed and instantly recognizable on the southeast corner of Kemp Avenue and Sycamore Lane. The front gable windows were removed, while the one on the side gable is now a vent. Most of the brackets are gone, but the porch is open, with the place retaining the ambiance of this 1911 postcard.

This group on Annie Hall's porch, believed to be at 21 Kemp Avenue, was photographed by Christopher Chandler on June 16, 1911, but the subjects are not identified.

This is Hap Handy's cottage at 89 Willow Street, in the actors' district. This simple Four Square dwelling could have been new when photographed in 1911. The porch is the only part of the exterior with notable change. It now has substantial posts, low walls around the edges, and a room built on the back of the east (right) side. A glimpse of 83 Willow is at left.

Alva Walling was born in 1900 in Keyport. She is seen in 1919 and in 1923 with her first husband, Connecticut native Leonard C. Fleckenstein. He was a real estate broker with extensive property interests in the Fair Haven area. An exempt member of the Fair Haven Fire Department, Fleckenstein died in 1938.

Leonard and Alva Fleckenstein had contractor George Hawkins build 12 Oak Place in 1927 for their family home. It is unchanged today.

Lois Pease Bodtmann is seen on the lawn of 12 Oak Place, *c.* 1929. Visible are the rear of 826 River Road (p. 35), unchanged, and the front of 825 River Road, with its porch now enclosed. Number 825 is retail space now, occupied by the Write Impression. Lois lent this and several fine other pictures.

Rufus S. Merritt's residence at 849 River Road is seen here in a view dated August 30, 1909. Merritt was a major real estate investor. This simple Vernacular Victorian house could be the one he built in 1882. The house is well-preserved today. The porch is unchanged, while there are minor modifications to the side-gabled ell, and the fence is gone.

The north side of Willow Street, east of Oak Place, is typical of the streets a maturing Fair Haven was developing at the turn of the century. These houses are unpretentious and constructed in traditional forms. This view of the block features numbers 77, 79, and 83 on a snowy February 23, 1911.

The same block viewed in December 1910 looking west includes number 89 Willow (see p. 37). The fields south of Willow would remain unbuilt for some years.

The Harvey M. Little Sr. house at the foot of Haggars Lane is seen *c.* 1900 over a footbridge crossing Fourth Creek, part of a lane connecting that street with Battin Road. The house, now painted red, is recognizable today. One exterior chimney exists in lieu of these three, while a new wing has been added to the north.

Cooney Terrace was cut during the development of the former Daniel F. Cooney property. The site, located on the Navesink River between Hance Road and Grange Avenue, was once held by Alfred F. Lichtenstein, who bought Red Gables on the Middletown shore instead of building a house he planned here. Peter J. Eichele hired Vincent J. Eck in 1929 to design this Dutch Colonial Revival at number 27. Reflecting the freedom of historical borrowing then, the Dutch-influenced house nevertheless contained a Palladian window. The Eicheles sold it to Dr. William Pearce in 1948.

Abe Bennett's Atlantic Hotel was built in 1889, the date of this image. It quickly became one of the major gathering places in town and was often patronized by a theatrical clientele. The stables in the rear were destroyed by fire in 1907. Comparing this image with that opposite makes one realize how well preserved the hotel was into modern times.

The Atlantic Hotel is seen looking north from its 121 Fair Haven Road locale *c.* 1907. The front-gabled building above the sidewalk crowd is gone, replaced by a parking lot. The porch was removed and a one-story extension was built on the south.

The Atlantic Hotel has been occupied in recent decades by several restaurants. Its old look is still retained in this 1976 image, but an unsympathetic remodeling has destroyed its nineteenth-century character, resulting in its removal from the Monmouth County Historic Sites Inventory. Nearly all of the old windows are gone, replaced with inappropriate contemporary shapes. A bay window replaced the Fair Haven Road entrance, while the side entrance has been built out.

Walter Van Horn purchased an old farmhouse near the northeast corner of Hance Road and Third Street prior to 1920, opening the Shady Knoll Hotel and Cottages. He added to his property, which was described in 1938—around the time of this postcard image—as having over 6 acres, some in flower and rock gardens, a main house, and three guest cottages with a total of over thirty bedrooms. The place is now a private residence on Third Street.

The family tradition of Bob Zerr of Rumson claims that this is the Sickler house on the west side of Fair Haven Road, opposite Clay Street, an extensively-changed structure that still stands. The image appears to be c. 1880s. Say BeeZee, I hope the story is true, as this is too great a picture to omit, the absence of a confirmed provenance notwithstanding.

Clay Street in winter around 1905 produced a scene both charming and puzzling, as the exact locale on this two-block street is not clear. It is a quintessential old Fair Haven street: narrow, compact, and little changed. (Collection of John Rhody.)

The northwest corner of Gillespie Avenue and Clay Street is unchanged since Christopher Chandler photographed it on February 15, 1911. The Italianate house at right, 53 Clay Street, William Trafford's in 1911, was probably moved there. Its style suggests a *c.* 1860s or 1870s origin, but the site is shown as vacant on the Fair Haven village plan in the 1889 Wolverton atlas. One wonders if it once belonged to Abram Trafford, postmaster when a Fair Haven post office was established in 1874, or Edmund Trafford, a storekeeper.

The William E. Kirk residence at 35 Clay Street is seen on September 14, 1909, at its northeast corner with De Normandie Avenue. It now has a one-bay extension on the east. The street is little changed; the mature trees are gone, with breaks in the pavement indicating their former presence. Kirk, a member of Fair Haven's first borough council, died in 1926. The house may have been built by John and Deborah Soden in the 1850s.

Fair Haven Road looking north from Clay Street today bears strong resemblance to the images depicted on this *c.* 1910 postcard. The readily recognizable house on the northeast corner, number 55 Fair Haven Road, is best known as the Edmund Wilber house. Wilber manufactured cigars at home after technological change forced the closing of the factory pictured on p. 68. (Collection of John Rhody.)

Donald Rankin, a native Scot and retired New York trucker, bought the Joyce house at 50 Fair Haven Road in the early 1890s. Robert D. Chandler-designed changes were made in 1895, likely including the addition of the octagonal tower. The view presented in this *c.* 1910 image is little changed today; even the well house is in place. Rankin, an early Fair Haven road supervisor, died in 1924.

John Van Tine bought the waterfront property east of the Fair Haven Road dock from Samuel T. Hendrickson in 1866, building the Van Tine Hotel, operating it for twenty years, and losing it by sheriff's sale in 1886. The property was later bought by Harry Van Tine. This and the image below date from 1962, the year of the building's destruction.

William Sperb bought the hotel in 1894 and made various improvements depicted in this photograph. One account that year claimed he gave away the old hotel and it was removed to another location. However, this appears to be an 1860s building. In more modern times, the hotel was vacant and owned by a builder who demolished it in 1962.

John Dowling built a 22-by-28-foot house at 718 River Road in late 1908, moving in the following February. George W. Smith was the carpenter for what appears to be the Queen Anne style's last hurrah in Fair Haven. The building was remodeled as offices. Despite a large addition in the rear and the enclosure of the porch, the former house is instantly recognizable today from this 1913 photograph by Christopher Chandler.

The vaudevillian Annie Hart had multiple houses in Fair Haven. This one at 660 River Road, seen in 1911 in a Christopher Chandler photograph, was built in the summer of 1909 when a news account called it one of the finest in the area. It was built by George Sewing of Red Bank, who also often designed his projects, for occupancy by "the merry widow." The house is well preserved today, although the widow's walk is gone, the porch has been enclosed, and the stairs have been narrowed.

This 1907 view was taken from the southeast corner of River Road and Maple Avenue by Christopher Chandler. The houses on the north side of River were new. The four visible are numbers 673, 675, 683, and 685 River Road. Note the brick pavement around the trolley tracks and the pedestrian in the distance walking on the bricks. Such pedestrians need to "dodge" approaching trolleys, and hence the sporting nickname "dodgers" in a city crossed by trolley lines, Brooklyn. The postcard version of this image deleted the telephone poles!

Christopher F. Cuttingham's fine Italianate house, perhaps built *c.* 1870, is seen on River Road in a 1910 image. No trace of it was found, but deed evidence indicates it should have been on the north side, in the block between De Normandie and Gillespie Avenues.

A riverfront lot west of the Fair Haven dock had been in the McAnerney family since 1887 when John bought 5.8 acres from James M. MacGregor. It was apparently unbuilt until Marshall McAnerney hired Robert D. Chandler in 1899 to design a 64-foot-square Colonial Revival house. Built by Arthur E. Smith of Fair Haven, completed in 1900, the house's east facade is seen in a Christopher D. Chandler photograph dated September 14, 1909.

The McAnerney house's relationship to the river is viewed in this 1909 image taken from the end of his dock. Note the attractive fence and bulkhead.

Jerome and Hannah Rice bought the McAnerney house in October 1926. The enclosure of the front porch is the only visible change since this *c.* 1930s image was taken. The house was demolished in November 1971 and three new houses were built on the site.

The billiard room in the old Rice house is seen *c.* 1930s. One does not want to move a pool table unnecessarily—the table was placed over the finished foundation of Newton Rice Jr.'s new house, with the structure completed around the table.

Newton Rice, born 1904, succeeded his father in the glove manufacturing business. He was a recreational horseman, preferring world traveling as a leisure pursuit. Rice died in 1980.

Jerome Rice, seen with son Newton in 1939, was a self-made glove manufacturer in New York. He and wife Hannah bought the McAnerney place in 1926. The two traveled the world, she following equestrian events.

Carmen Kahn, born 1910 in Cincinnati, Ohio, is a graduate of the University of Cincinnati. Seen here in the summer of 1932, she married Newton Rice and still lives on the estate held by the family since 1926.

This photograph of the Rice children on the shore in front of their home *c.* 1940s provides an opportunity to observe a wide beach, one much eroded since. Joan stands above Jerry, while brother Newton is at right.

Joan Rice, daughter of Newton and Carmen, learned to sit a horse early. Her grandmother Hannah, who traveled extensively with her horse, had Joan riding before she walked. Joan was a recreational equestrian.

The caretakers' house on the Rice estate is still standing, now a private residence behind Fairwater Lane, a new street opened after the old house was demolished. The rock garden was by Berardi of Little Silver. This image is c. 1930s.

The Grand View Hotel, located on the west side of Fair Haven Road at the Navesink shore adjacent to the Rice property, was bought by Jerome Rice in 1935 and demolished for an expansion of his grounds. The place had numerous owners over the years, including a group of New York postal employees in the 1920s. This view is from a c. 1907 postcard.

Coverts Cove is on the stem of the Fair Haven shore east of the yacht club, near the Rumson border. It is viewed here in 1907.

The Parker homestead, built around the middle of the nineteenth century, still stands at 304 Fair Haven Road, not recognizable after expansion. The place was later owned by George Ingraham, who developed the surrounding area. Some of the subjects can be identified by matching them with those below. The pictures were taken on the same day c. early 1880s.

The patriarch of the Parker family is Daniel (1814–1885), with the white beard at right. His wife, Mary Springsteen Parker (1821–1894), is to his right. The others, clockwise from lower left, are Adele (Addie) Parker (later Gledhill), an unidentified baby, Matilda Dwight Parker (wife of Charles), Mary Catherine Parker Hammer, Isabel Parker (later Longstreet), Frank Hammer, Charles Parker (1844–1910, great-grandfather of the lender, Richard F. Doughty), and an unidentified child with a fancy collar.

William Doughty built this substantial Four Square at 136 Hance Road, at its southwest corner with First Avenue, *c*. 1910. Mike Jacobs, the noted prizefight promoter, later lived here. He sold it in 1946, by which time he owned the famed William Bingham house on Bingham Hill (see *Rumson*, p. 112). The house is well-preserved, with the porch's enclosure its only substantive change.

This late-nineteenth-century image from the Chandler collection lacks identification, but likely pictures one of Fair Haven's earliest houses.

The Lemon and Lewis places—seen here on January 1, 1910—are two of the old west Fair Haven riverfront estates.

Houses belonging to the McClure family are seen on Fair Haven's western shore in 1910.

Horace P. Cook bought about 10.5 acres of the former James MacGregor estate in 1906, hiring Red Bank architect Fred Truex to design this fine Colonial Revival house on the Navesink River, adjacent to Fourth Creek. A private community around a single street, both called Riverlawn, developed. The house, at 77 Riverlawn Drive, is viewed from the west in 1908.

The Cook house is viewed from McAnerney's dock (p. 50) in 1909. Cook kept the place briefly, selling in 1910 to Dudley Farrand of Newark. Riverlawn development accelerated in the 1920s and 1930s, a period when several Colonial Revival houses were built.

Theodore F. White bought a 25-acre tract of Borden Hance's farm in 1892 and platted it for division as house lots. It is located in Fair Haven's western section, but called East Side Park as the area was east of the town of Red Bank, where it would be marketed as new suburban building lots. This 1949 aerial view shows the westernmost part of East Side Park bordering Schwenkers Pond.

Sandi von Pier, a lifelong East Side Park resident, designs web pages and other artistic creations. Seen here in a 1983 self-portrait during her leather and Spandex days with Schwenkers Pond in the background, Sandi proudly showed off her first car, a 1980 Camaro.

River Road runs along the top of the picture, while First Street parallels it below, running east from the curving Chestnut Street. White sold a third of his East Side Park lots in two years, moving there himself. This 1949 aerial shows a mature, developed section, but since then, house expansion and new construction have covered even more of the ground.

Pauline Denhart's house obviously had a well-built chimney, as that was the only part standing following a 1909 fire.

John F. James built this Colonial Revival in 1909 on the site of the Denhart house at 92 Grange Avenue. His contractor was George W. Sewing of Red Bank, who often designed his projects. The house measured 44 by 54 feet. Both pictures on this page are *c.* 1910.

The interior focal point of the James house was a 26-by-30-foot reception room on the north, now the living room. A *New Jersey Standard* account of April 2, 1909, indicated the first floor "will be finished in mission wood, weathered oak and mahogany and the second floor in white enamel and mahogany."

Joseph E. Meyer, who bought the James house in 1918, reportedly made costly improvements, also done by Sewing, but the exterior in this 1933 image appears little changed. Meyer raced horses and built a sizable stable to house them. The property has since been reduced by sale, while there is adjacent new construction.

A view of the dining room table may not be an appropriate image under which to mention that Meyer was a chicken fancier, as his were exhibition birds. He was awarded first prizes at the Trenton State Fair. The house remains in a fine state of preservation, with most street-visible changes minor. Alterations have been made in the rear. This image is *c.* 1930s.

This 1909 image shows McClures Point and cove at the foot of Grange Avenue. Formerly named Pintards Point for the family long holding it, the spot was renamed for David McClure, a noted New York lawyer who declined a judgeship to remain in practice. McClure bought his waterfront property *c.* 1880, erecting a large frame house.

The McClures Point Colonial Revival, now at 167 Grange Avenue, is on an estate that was given at least three names by former owners beginning the 1930s: Round Point, Hard-a-Lee, and Windward. It is not clear if McClure's house was largely rebuilt in 1940 or replaced in its entirety. This recent view of the long house shows its two gables projecting toward the Navesink River. (A Scott Longfield photograph.)

Three
Places to Work

The Fair Haven Shopping Center on the south side of River Road, seen here *c*. 1953, was designed by Bernard Kellenyi for Allen Brothers around 1953. Two other Kellenyi commissions are part of this scene today. Free-standing stores were built *c*. 1959 to the right of the strip, and a bank was constructed west (to the right in this photograph) of the service station, *c*. 1967. The shopping center's off-street parking reflects Fair Haven's response to a more mobile society. Reflecting current travel and shopping patterns, some think of the shops as a town center.

The Atlantic Highlands Gas Company, a predecessor of the New Jersey Natural Gas Company, was laying gas lines along River Road in early 1911. The company's crew was photographed opposite Church Street on March 15. Although this stretch seems to be a clear ditch, workers struck a large oak stump in front of John Bennett's grocery store.

Squire William Curchin was a carpenter by trade. He was also a barber, initially opening his shop only on Wednesday nights and Saturdays, but later full-time. This shop seen c. 1910s was on the west side of Fair Haven Road, south of River Road, adjacent to the former firehouse. The building was later a library and a police station. The Curchin family pictures were lent by Kenneth, a grandson of the squire, all of whose sons were taught the barbering trade. However, only Ken of his generation practiced the trade, the fifth to do so.

Alfred Hendrickson's team and crew paused on River Road for Christopher Chandler's camera on March 10, 1911. Note that a load, apparently furniture, is protected by a canvas cover, which gives a small wagon the appearance of a substantial truck.

Number 772 River Road was built as Liberty Hall at an unspecified date in the nineteenth century. The building has been greatly changed by expansions and alterations. The hall was used for a variety of public gatherings, including meetings, dances, and athletic events. The front of the building, shown here on a c. 1940 postcard, has been changed, with the corner at right cut away for a new entrance.

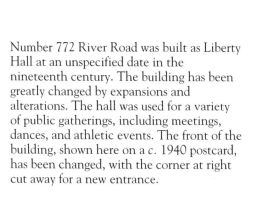

Edmund H. Wilber's cigar-manufacturing facility was a famed Fair Haven male gathering place. Located on the northeast corner of River and Fair Haven Roads, it was widely known by its nickname, the Eel Pot. Wilber was born 1856 in Missouri, but spent most of his life in Fair Haven, moving here as a youth. He learned the cigar-making trade in New York under his brother William Henry, opening his business in Fair Haven after a brief spell in Massachusetts. The building was moved a short distance to the east when the service station on p. 71 was built. Cigar-making machines forced Wilber to close his plant not long after this summer of 1910 image was taken, but he continued to make cigars at home (see p. 46). Wilber died in 1936.

An impatient cat, Justice of the Peace William Curchin, and George J. Hendrickson stand in front of the latter's general store at the northwest corner of River and Fair Haven Roads in 1912. The Hendricksons had operated a store for about seventy years, but changing retail and travel patterns caused them to plan its closing on February 22, 1918. However, it was destroyed by fire early that morning, with reports of underinsurance dampening the author's usual suspicions.

Charles Worthly, Fair Haven's first policeman, is in front of the ruins of the Hendrickson general store following the February 22, 1918, fire. The site is now Victory Memorial Park

The William Bennetts opened an ice cream parlor in June 1909 in the former saloon of the North Shrewsbury Hotel at the southeast corner of River and Fair Haven Roads. They wired the place for electric lights and it quickly became popular as a meeting place for the young. The sign on the canopy was deleted when this Christopher Chandler photograph was made into a printed postcard.

Christopher Chandler's store was on the southwest corner of River and Fair Haven Roads. It included the post office during his tenure as postmaster. Chandler began occupancy as a tenant of George Hendrickson, but bought the building in 1909, altering it for his expanding postal and retail operations.

Bob Cameron's Esso station, seen here *c.* 1940, was on the northeast corner of River and Fair Haven Roads. Bob Pettigrew was on the right bench at the right time when this photograph was taken, preserving his image for generations to come.

An A.& P. store was on the north side of River Road, east of Fair Haven Road. This image was taken *c.* 1930s, a time when a grocery store could locate in the midst of a "downtown" shopping area with no thought to available parking space.

The Candlelight Gift Shop is seen in a 1940s postcard at its original location at the north side of River Road adjacent to the post office. (Collection of John Rhody.)

The Candlelight Gift Shop was moved from the north to the south side of River Road in 1947. It now stands at 770 River Road, with an enclosed porch around the front, occupied by Fairwinds Deli.

Henry R. Stadler opened a tavern and restaurant at the former DeSotolongo house at 740 River Road in July 1939. A brick and cement addition was built perhaps in 1942 when the Willowbrook Inn was opened as an annex to the tavern. It is seen here on a 1940s postcard. The building today houses the Fair Haven Commons retail shops, with the original house barely visible amidst further additions that have greatly expanded the complex.

THE GREEN SHUTTER, FAIR HAVEN, N.J.

The Green Shutter at 771 River Road was a residence remodeled as an antique shop when this postcard was published around 1940. It is retail space today, little changed from the older image.

This mid-1960s view of Miller's Exxon at the southeast corner of River Road and Smith Street shows many changes, including the name. The large-letter sign is gone, as is the rental car operation, while the pumps are no longer as close to the street. The third bay on the east, not present on p. 65, was added c. 1962; the entire station was replaced in 1967.

Edgar J. Bacigalupi had a Jacobsen Mower Agency on Forman Place, covering Monmouth, Ocean, and Middlesex Counties. This image is from the 1939 *Jersey Shore Pictorial*.

The presence of this double store at 604 and 606 River Road is not readily apparent today, but the angled doors provide a clue through major changes. This early 1950s image shows new television and butcher stores, which have been replaced by the Riverside Salon and Rainbow 1-Hour Photo-finishing. A pitched roof with a gabled front hampers casual identification. The former house at right, now the offices of Drs. Nickel and Gardiner, provides additional evidence for the skeptic.

One wonders how many third-world countries do not eat as well as the average American pet dog. In the event one thinks the pampered pooch originated in the television age, be mindful that Harold Dowstra's Canine Kitchen and Boarding Kennel delivered catered meals to dogs made from fresh beef in the 1930s. Meals were customized to suit individual needs. Dowstra's place was the former Rumson Farm Kennels on Buena Vista Avenue, near River Road. This image is from a 1937 *Monmouth Pictorial*.

Leonard Fleckenstein built his FFF Service Station for investment operation in 1928 at 823 River Road, at its northeast corner with Gillespie Avenue. The station was demolished in August 1981. Note the exterior lifts and the pump with a visible-flow operation.

The Store on River Road, number 823 at the northeast corner of Gillespie Avenue, is the only historic district store with off-street parking as it is set back on the former gas station space. The non-revealing name intends to provoke curiosity, reflecting eclectic, changing merchandise. Opened in 1983 by Mara and Tim Neske, college-trained potters, and seen here when new, the store sells products that can not be categorized as furniture, gifts, or decorative accessories, and yet are all three. The Neskes initially had a downstairs pottery studio, although current pottery lines are bought from others.

Four
Community Life

Local officials are posing at a c. 1910s election in the Fair Haven firehouse. Harvey Little Jr. is standing at right. Note the fire apparatus at left and in the rear and the harness hanging from the ceiling.

Fair Haven's first school district was formed in 1841, the year a school was reported built on the eastern stem of River Road. A larger room over a store was later used. The pictured school, built in 1878 on Willow Street, is seen around the time of its completion. The former school and lot were auctioned on May 24, 1879, and sold to Forman Smith for $25. The property was expanded and used as a shop by Forman's sons, local builders, near his home at 867 River Road.

The building at top was expanded twice, with two rooms added c. 1888 and 1898. One might be able to "see" the original building, notably the gabled end at right, in this c. 1908 postcard in the absence of the trees. This school lasted long after its expected life span, in use until its demolition c. 1934 for the new Willow Street School, now the Viola L. Sickles School.

PUBLIC SCHOOL, FAIR HAVEN, N

A new Willow Street School, with elements of Moderne design incorporated by architect J. Noble Pierson & Son, was opened in 1935 on the site of the earlier school. It was built in part by Works Progress Administration funds. The school is seen *c*. 1940s, in a view made prior to the addition of a wing on the west (left) *c*. 1955. (Collection of John Rhody.)

The Willow Street School was renamed in 1973 in honor of Viola L. Sickles, who retired as principal in 1961 at age seventy-one, after a fifty-two year career which she began as a teacher following her 1909 graduation from Trenton Normal School. She is seen in December 1981 with Superintendent Robert Chartier at a ceremony unveiling her name in aluminum letters.

The Knollwood School, designed in the Colonial Revival style, was built on the west side of Hance Road and opened in 1925. A twelve-unit addition was attached to the west in 1950, designed by Pierson and MacWilliam. Eight classrooms and a multi-purpose room were added in 1955, reflecting expanding enrollment that impacted the entire region. This image from 1975 shows the completed building.

Lynn Carter, born in 1944, received her elementary education in the Fair Haven system. She won the Borden Scholarship at Rumson-Fair Haven Regional High School, graduating from Vassar and later earning a Master of Arts at the University of Hawaii.

A procession of kindergarten students holding a rope chain to guide and control the crowd is proceeding on Hance Road to the former youth center. Diane Smith (now Carmona), lender of the picture, is pictured in the front center between Frank Buchanan and Bob McLellan. Her mother and brother Jay are present at right on the first day of school in September 1965.

The first Fair Haven colored school was erected in 1881 amidst controversy over the use of public funds for building schools for specific groups. Fair Haven and Shrewsbury Township were in the vanguard of New Jersey's segregated educational practices, which lasted into the 1950s. The first school was destroyed by an incendiary fire in 1926. It was replaced by the second Fisk Street School, at number 37, shown here in 1953 when it was being converted into a community activity center. It was later vacant, but on October 10, 1983, following a remodeling by Red Bank architects Kaplan, Gaunt, and De Santis, the former school was rededicated as a police headquarters and youth center. (The Dorn's Collection.)

The proud graduates of the Fair Haven School around 1926 include Elizabeth Chandler La Bau Willis (second from right in the center), who is the mother of the lender, Marilyn Willis.

Fair Haven Troop #1 of the Boy Scouts of America, c. 1910, are a well-outfitted, eager bunch of boys. How about those shirts? With four large pockets, they are prepared to return from a field trip with all manner of stuff. However, this is not the origin of the "deep pocket" doctrine.

The Bethel A.M.E. Church founded in 1858 was the origin of the Fisk Chapel A.M.E. Church. The congregation built this Stick Style-Gothic edifice at 38 Fisk Street in 1882, replacing an earlier structure. Funds and land were provided by General Clinton B. Fisk, a Rumson resident widely known for his benefactions to African-Americans, including the money to found Fisk University in Tennessee. The chapel, dedicated on August 20, 1882, is seen in 1974 on its original site.

The congregation planned to erect a modern church, as the old one no longer met its needs by the early 1970s. The church was offered to the borough to avoid its destruction, but the ancient edifice would need to be relocated. Duffy Fisher of Middletown, a renowned building mover who often moved structures single-handedly, was engaged. The building was cut in two for the trip in June 1975 to its new home at 25 Cedar Street.

The Fisk congregation broke ground on July 28, 1974, for its new church designed by Floyd Scott of Kellenyi Associates. Present at the ceremony were Bishop Ernest L. Hickman, Mayor Robert A. Matthews, and the Reverend Herschel A. Mosley.

The building's historic stature was recognized by its listing on the National Register of Historic Places in 1975. A fire in June 1976 marred plans for its new use as a community center.

Construction of the modern Fisk
A.M.E. Church was delayed to
November 1975. The finished building
was dedicated on July 17, 1976.
Present were the pastor, the Reverend
Herschel A. Mosley, the Right
Reverend Richard A. Hildebrand
(who delivered the principal sermon),
and Fair Haven Mayor W.R. Ed Kiely.

The relocated Fisk Chapel was renamed
Bicentennial Hall and dedicated on
September 18, 1976, Fair Haven's
Bicentennial Day. A cornerstone was laid,
the building was presented to the borough
by the Reverend Mosley, and the
restoration committee introduced, led by
Bicentennial Committee Chairman
Charles Gompert. The building is used for
a variety of civic organizations, including
historical groups.

The Fair Haven Fire Department was founded in March 1904, its organization prompted by the ineffectiveness of bucket brigades in fighting a Haggars Lane house fire. Incorporation followed that June. Many well-known Fair Haven names were among the incorporators, including Christopher D. Chandler, who photographed the firehouse the members built on Fair Haven Road at an unspecified date, presumably not long after the founding of the group.

Susan Donaldson's yoga studio is representative of the current occupants of the former firehouse. It is located at 120 Fair Haven Road, is known as the Meyer Building, and has been remodeled for use as offices. Susan teaches a form of gentle yoga addressing the discipline's basic aim of linking body and mind in a state of spiritual insight that emphasizes relaxation, tension reduction, and a flexible body. (A Danny Sanchez portrait.)

Fair Haven's early fire alarm consisted of a traditional rim from a locomotive wheel, which, when struck gong-fashion with a sledgehammer, could be heard for some distance. The locals gathered proudly around the new bell in early 1909, as shown in this often-illustrated postcard.

This is a *c.* 1910 image of an early hook-and-ladder truck. Motorized equipment was first purchased in 1920. The new company was tested early, as a fire in March 1907 destroyed the Atlantic Hotel stables, killing seven horses and threatening the village's business district.

Concrete footings and a foundation were built in early February 1909. David H. Bennett was to complete the 75-foot tower in about a week, after which electrical apparatus would be installed. The tower was placed in the rear of the firehouse lot, while the bell was in a ready position during construction.

Christopher Chandler was present on February 22, 1909, to photograph the raising of the bell, a 30-minute process. The bell would be painted that September by four members of the company. This view provides a distant but useful glimpse of River and Fair Haven Roads. Hendrickson's store (p. 69) is at left, while the side of Chandler's post office building is the one-and-one-half-story, end-gabled building behind the tower. Mechanics Hall, also known as Monmouth Hall, is at right, while a glimpse of the residence at 93 Fair Haven Road is in the distance.

The 75th anniversary of the Fair Haven Fire Company was celebrated on June 2, 1979, with a parade that attracted over fifty-five companies. The award for longest distance traveled went to the group from Fair Haven, New York, but it seems only fair to mention that the Fair Haven, Massachusetts, crew came quite a distance, too. The celebrations continued into the night on the fairgrounds.

The firemen's fair, an annual week-long event in August, is the largest public gathering in Fair Haven. Rides, food, and games of chance are the current staples of the event held adjacent to the present River Road firehouse. These boys were contemplating their next ride in 1976.

The firemen's fair is one of Fair Haven's oldest traditions, dating from the early years of the company. A *c.* 1910 event would have featured entertainment from the many vaudevillians in town and dancing. The event was earlier held on the former fairgrounds adjacent to the firehouse, including what later became the site of the borough hall. This is a glimpse of the 1972 fair.

Fair Haven Day was a two-day celebration on Saturday and Sunday, July 22–23, 1939. Theodore J. Labrecque, then a Red Bank lawyer, is seen speaking of the town's accomplishments at the firemen's fairgrounds. He is flanked by mayors. At left are Charles R. English of Red Bank, Walter J. Sweeney of Sea Bright, and Oliver Frake of Little Silver. Fair Haven's Arthur Sickles is at right.

The Church of the Nativity was founded in 1953, taking over part of the overcrowded St. James parish of Red Bank. Their Colonial Revival edifice, seating seven hundred, is located on the east side of Hance Road, near the north side of Ridge Road. It was begun in late 1953 and was opened and blessed on February 13, 1955. The rectory was built at the same time, while a parish hall was added in 1990.

The Knights of Columbus meeting hall is a remodeled former bottling plant on Third Street west of Fair Haven Road. It is seen in 1972 at the time of its dedication.

Episcopal worship at Fair Haven began in the early 1880s. A *Register* announcement on February 20, 1884, of an Ash Wednesday service to be held at Liberty Hall was its first public notice. The cornerstone of the original Chapel of the Holy Communion was laid on November 3, 1884. The building, erected at the southeast corner of River Road and Church Street, is a combination of the Shingle and Stick Styles prominent at the time; its architect is unknown.

The church was then a mission of St. George's in Rumson. Its first service was the Eucharist celebrated by the Reverend Dr. Benjamin Franklin, rector of Christ Church in Shrewsbury, on Wednesday, August 19, 1885. The chapel was consecrated on Tuesday, September 8, 1885, by the Right Reverend Dr. John Scarborough, Bishop of New Jersey. This magnificent, rare interior view dates from that period.

The number of Holy Communion recipients grew under the Reverends Christopher Snyder (1942–1955) and Charles L. Wood (1956–58), resulting in the attainment of parish status in 1958. The congregation was incorporated that year as the Episcopal Church of the Holy Communion. The Reverend Donald A. MacLeod was appointed its first rector. Structural problems are reflected in this early 1960s image, with the tower then removed. The building was replaced with the present edifice in 1968.

The Reverend Frederick E. Preuss II, after serving several years as rector of the Church of the Holy Communion, left in 1972, making a stark career change. He joined St. Aiden's, a church in an isolated area in Vermont that was modeled after Lindisfarne, the monastery and bishopric established by St. Aiden in 635 on an island of the same name off the east coast of Northumbria. The venture was short-lived and Frederick Preuss later left the church.

Methodism in Fair Haven originated in 1843 with early worshipers meeting at a local school under the leadership of the Reverend Bartine Twiford. A small church was begun in 1852. This Stick Style edifice was designed by Robert D. Chandler and built around 1884 at 786 River Road. The lower level was used as a hall and Sunday school.

The Methodist church was remodeled following its purchase by the Moxley-Abacus Lodge No. 78 of the F. & A. Masons, a group with origins in Long Branch. The building appears new when viewed from its Colonial Revival north facade. However, its origins can be readily seen when looking at the five bays on the side. The masons donated the bell, once housed in the former tower, to the Methodist church, where it was mounted on the ground at their present location (p. 96) and dedicated as a memorial to Obadiah Hallenbake.

The Christian Endeavor, a Methodist youth group and education society, is seen outside the River Road church in 1930. The tall boy in the left rear is still around town standing over his contemporaries. He is Wesley Crozier, who is now the church's historian. Virginia Smith Paine lent the picture, preserving her own image fourth from left in front. Evelyn Bennett is to her left.

Wes, Ginny, and Evelyn are also represented in the Christian Endeavor's 1937 photograph. He is third from the left, at top, while Ginny is fourth from the left at bottom. Evelyn is at right, in the middle with the floral print dress. Barbara Hunting is at right on the bottom.

The United Methodist Christ Church, located on a lane north of Ridge Road surrounded by Fair Haven Fields, is seen in a c. 1963 image when the edifice was nearing completion. The architects were William Kendall Albert and Oren R. Thomas of Pennsauken, New Jersey. It is not visible from the street, prompting some to call it "Fair Haven's best secret." The Fair Haven Methodist Church merged with Goodwill Methodist of Rumson, which had a declining enrollment, and relocated from its longtime River Road location (p. 94).

This late 1920s image is of a Fair Haven Arbor Day celebration.

The Lovett Nursery field on the north side of Ridge Road west of Fair Haven Road is seen here in 1953. The borough purchased about 77 acres twenty years later with Green Acres funds, turning it into the present Fair Haven Fields park and recreation area.

Patriotic fervor following the end of the Great War was expressed in Fair Haven on May 11, 1919, Mothers Day and the six-month anniversary of the armistice. A commemorative service flag honoring the veterans was hung across River Road along with a number of smaller flags; it was later flown on the lot vacated by the destruction of Hendrickson's store (p. 69). A permanent memorial would follow.

On July 4, 1919, there was an outpouring of patriotic honor showered upon returned soldiers in a town-wide welcome home. The place was packed with visitors and most buildings were decorated. Entertainment included aerial stunts by two flyers and one steeplejack. A parade followed, with this image the Italian brass band of Red Bank. The permanent memorial was five years away.

A local committee organized to pay for a memorial park by private subscription with a fund-raising goal of $10,000. The site of the destroyed store was bought from the Hendrickson estate for $5,000. A large doughboy monument and granite base, which arrived early in 1924, cost $1,925. They were stored while the site was prepared, including landscaping and the erection of walks and electric light posts. Community support was broad, both in Fair Haven and surrounding towns.

The statue was dedicated on August 16, 1924. A parade from Lake Avenue to the eastern end of town, led by marshal Dr. Edwin F. Stewart, began the major celebration. There were a number of speeches in the park. A bronze plaque on the base is inscribed with the names of forty-nine Fair Havenites who served in the war. Two, Christopher Doughty and Walter Grover, were killed in action, while Charles Burdge, Chester Berry, and Myron Morson died in service. The statue was unveiled by Mrs. Edward Doughty, Christopher's mother.

The Spirit of the Doughboy, one of many replicas of a design sculpted by E.N. Viqueney of Americus, Georgia, was installed with a gun in his left hand and a hand grenade in his right fist. Those parts, which disappeared unexplainably many years ago, were the subject of a search in the early 1990s. The statue is seen here following the 1994 Memorial Day Parade, prior to restoration of the missing parts. The monument visible to the right of the doughboy honors ten Fair Haven residents who gave their lives in World War II and one who was killed in the Korean War. A second monument (not visible here) on the grounds honors all Fair Haven residents who served their country in the armed forces. The flag was donated by the Fair Haven Volunteer Fire Company in honor of those who served. (A Scott Longfield photograph.)

Five
Around Town

The six Chandler brothers, sons of John Henry Chandler, a mariner, are seen c. 1890s. They are, from left to right, Louis, Robert, Charles, Benjamin, Christopher, and William. Christopher's varied interests included photography. He published local view postcards, with his work providing an in-depth pictorial record of Fair Haven in the years around 1910. His oeuvre is liberally illustrated in this book, with only some images identified as his. Robert was a notable architect and boat builder. Some of his commissions are found herein; his iceboats were among the fastest on the Navesink and included the legendary *Scud*.

These well outfitted but unidentified local bicycle enthusiasts from the turn of the century reflect the popularity of this recreational activity. Traveling in groups, often organized under the League of American Wheelmen, bicyclists were an effective force in campaigning for better roads. There are probably one or more Chandlers in this gathering, the photograph coming from a family collection.

The first car on the Monmouth County Electric Company trolley line left Red Bank around 1:30 pm on January 1, 1907, guided by superintendent John Gaul with a number of officials on board. It was greeted in Fair Haven by a crowd of about one hundred residents, with two stops made due to the accumulation of mud on the tracks. The return trip took twelve minutes, with two stops made to take on passengers. (Collection of John Rhody.)

These unidentified drivers in livery were seen around Fair Haven c. 1915.

The local kids gave the Sickles' dog's litter a wagon ride in 1931. They were photographed at the corner of River Road and De Normandie Avenue in front of Frank Snyder's home, with the Methodist parsonage in the background. They are Ronald Sickles, Donald Snyder, Virginia Smith Paine (who preserved the image), Paul Smith, and possibly Joan Snyder.

Cornelia Stevenson Kirkman, born in 1858 in Brooklyn, married Frank Augustus Mulford, a native of Patchogue, New York, born in 1854. They lived over thirty years on De Normandie Avenue and had three children, including the famed racing driver, Ralph Mulford. Frank, known as "Old Judge Mulford," was a teacher and principal at the Highlands School, and principal at Lakewood. His nickname came from his local position of justice of the peace; he also served Fair Haven as recorder. The picture was lent by a granddaughter, Virginia Frances Smith Paine.

Ralph Kirkman Mulford, born 1884 in Brooklyn, moved at age ten to Fair Haven where he developed an early interest in automobiles. He operated a Red Bank trucking business as a youth. He is pictured in 1911 with his wife, Ethel. Mulford attained fame as an automobile racer, and was the subject of a disputed finish at the first Indianapolis 500 race in 1911. He claimed to have finished first, but was denied victory because the officials did not properly count his laps, preferring that first place be awarded to the local driver of an Indianapolis-made car, the Marmon.

Ralph Mulford worked for Lozier and is closely identified with their automobile. He is shown here in 1911 with his mechanic (who usually rode with the driver then), another Fair Havenite, Will Chandler. Mulford did not "win" an Indianapolis 500, but finished in the top ten six times in nine attempts. This image is a real photo postcard inscribed by Ethel, "We are bringing home the Vanderbilt Cup." (With thanks to Ralph Mulford Jr.)

The Vanderbilt, a long-distance road race in Savannah, Georgia, was won by Mulford on November 27, 1911. He excelled in long-distance races, many of which were run over twenty-four hours. Mulford was AAA national champion for 1911 and 1918. He also raced in mountain climbing competitions, holding world records for ascents up Pikes Peak, Mount Washington, Mount Wilson, and Mount Baldy. Mulford was elected to the Automobile Racing Hall of Fame. He died in Massachusetts in 1973.

This *c.* 1909 view of the corner of Fair Haven Road and Willow Street looking south resembles the present landscape, but with pointed change. The gate, now an entrance to McCarter Park, is no longer a portal to a private road to the Thomas McCarter estate. The street is paved, so a McCarter no longer has to plow it up and give it a coating of stone, as Thomas did in 1917. The house at right still stands, little changed with the exception of the porch.

Thomas N. McCarter's vast estate called Rumson Hill spanned that borough and Fair Haven, although it was bought before either municipality was formed. The house was built in 1906-7 in Rumson, but a main entrance was in Fair Haven, as noted at the top of the page. According to an October 31, 1906 *Register* account, McCarter contemplated calling his estate Rumsonhaven, a name coined by the combination of Rumson Road and Fair Haven. This entrance, seen in a *c.* 1907 Chandler postcard, is on Willow Street. Similar Rumson Hill gateposts stand farther south on Fair Haven Road, and on Rumson Road.

Thomas McCarter's three-and-one-half-story Georgian Revival mansion, designed by Warrington G. Lawrence and built in 1905-6, stood in Rumson, but his grounds included extensive Fair Haven acreage. Christopher Chandler's November 28, 1909 photograph is titled "Reflections Rumson Hill Lake."

McCarter's Fair Haven grounds included land bordered today by Willow, Fair Haven, and Rumson Roads and Kemp Avenue. Part of the grounds were wooded in McCarter's time, as evidenced in this November 28, 1909 Chandler photograph.

River Road looking east on November 4, 1907, has two prominent business buildings on either side. Wilber's cigar plant (p. 68) is at left, while the North Shrewsbury Hotel is at right. The steeple of the Methodist church (p. 94) is visible above Liberty Hall. (Collection of Joseph Eid.)

Lois England Brett found the elk in the rear of Victory Memorial Park a convenient perch, while today it gives us a view of the corner of River and Fair Haven Roads, c. 1930. She is accompanied by her father, one-time fire chief Lester England, and Eva Huff Little, his mother-in-law. The elk is believed to have been taken down in the 1930s.

River Road appeared quiet on snowy January 15, 1910, with the view looking east. The trolley was running through the snow.

One did not need a regulation course for a croquet game c. 1940. Elizabeth Chandler Willis is at right, with companions in front of 678 River Road. Numbers 673 and 675 (left and right) appear in the background.

This c. 1907 postcard glimpse of the river from the foot of Fair Haven Road differs from the present landscape. The lawn and street are now level and houses have been built on the VanTine Hotel grounds at right. The dock is visible today from a similar point in the street.

The Jersey Central Power & Light substation on the north side of Ridge Road, east of Hance Road, is seen here in a 1959 rendering by Bernard Kellenyi's office. Although not a house, it was designed to look like one. It fooled at least one passer-by at a critical time. Fair Haven was not eager to have a substation and did not embrace the initial "modern" design. Kellenyi changed the style to appeal "Colonial" and added decorative elements for the building to appear residential. He learned the disguise worked when a friend reported seeing a stranded motorist knocking at the door for help.

PEARL STREET, (Looking North.) FAIR HAVEN, N.-J.

The corners at Fair Haven Road, looking north from River Road, have changed since this c. 1910 postcard view. Hendrickson's two-story store on the west (left) was destroyed by fire in 1918 (p. 69). Wilber's cigar plant on the east (p. 68) is replaced by the Corner Café. Much of the balance of the tree-shaded street still resembles its appearance of nearly nine decades ago.

The Memorial Day Parade of May 25, 1981, advancing north on Fair Haven Road and turning west on River Road, provides a glimpse of major change in a brief period. The gas station, which opened as a Gulf franchise, was replaced by a bank. The town no longer has a drug store, since the Fair Haven Pharmacy moved to the western stem of River Road, later closing in 1996. The adjacent Fair Haven Hardware, founded in 1945 by James La Bau, expanded, taking the corner space. The former Atlantic Hotel is in the background.

The shore near Fourth Creek (p. 130), at left, is viewed westward to a spot east of Hance Road in a c. 1969 aerial by John Lentz. The mouth of the creek suggests its navigable past, but most cross it over River Road (west of Fair Haven Road) and by then, it is a tiny stream. The future Fair Haven Fields was still an open lot, with Christ Church (p. 96) and the power substation

(p. 110) visible near the top. The offices were not built around Cedar Street, near the fold, with the lot west of the firehouse occupied by a drive-in restaurant. McCarters Pond is at the upper left, while a gas station was still on the southeast corner of River and Fair Haven Roads.

William Curchin, whose son William would be known by the honorific "Squire," moved to Red Bank in the late 1850s, but returned to Brooklyn when his barber shop was not successful. He enlisted in the Union Army and served until 1865, when he was discharged, having contracted typhoid fever, only to discover he had lost his wife. In 1866 he settled in Fair Haven to improve his health. He opened a barber shop here and remarried, being joined by his son in 1873. The elder Curchin is seen here late in life.

Squire William, seen here with wife, Melvina Curchin, c. late 1920s, was long part of early Fair Haven's public life, beginning with his involvement in the campaign to secure borough status c. 1911. He was a founder of the Fair Haven Fire Department in 1904. He was tax assessor for many years; his awareness of forthcoming tax sales allowed him to secure a sizable real estate portfolio. The squire, as justice of the peace, handled many Saturday night abuse complaints from women with drunken husbands. His advice: wait until Monday.

Squire William Curchin was long-lived and prolific. Born in 1849 in Williamsburg, Brooklyn, he is seen in the center with wife Melvina at his 70th birthday party. The couple had fourteen children. She was his father's second wife's granddaughter. Readers may determine the dual relationship between this husband and wife, unless they are reading, as the author is writing, too late at night to think.

Not every member of the handsome Curchin clan is identified, but we know Lester and his wife, Beatrice Jones Curchin, are at the bottom. Anna Mabel Hayden Curchin and Lilly Curchin are in the middle, but the woman to the right is unknown. Alonzo Smith Curchin and Alex are at top, but the man at right is unknown.

One would not expect it, but this face had a long career, both on the vaudeville stage and in Fair Haven public life. Tony Hunting came to the area as a youth in his father's circus in which he had varied jobs, including driving the circus mascot (a goat) which pulled a sulky. He had an act with his wife, and the two were known as Hunting and Francis. Hunting was a theater owner and manager in Red Bank. His public positions in Fair Haven included the mayoralty. (Collection of Karen L. Schnitzspahn.)

Bessie Stimson, a well-known local vaudevillian, is seen holding a doll. (Collection of Karen L. Schnitzspahn.)

Hazel Frances Mulford, born in 1897, was a daughter of Franklin and Cornelia Mulford and brother of Ralph (p. 104). She is pictured in Fair Haven with her grandfather Ralph Kirkman, a Brooklyn building contractor, c. 1903. Hazel married Howard P. Smith in 1918. Their three children include Virginia Frances Smith Paine, the lender of this photograph.

It has been said that long-married couples sometimes come to look like one another. However, Charles Hayden and Olive Curchin Hayden may have been destined for each other, as they have an uncanny resemblance at a young age.

Mrs. James La Bau (nee Woodward), the daughter of a minister of Christ Church in Middletown, lived on the southeast corner of River and Hance Roads and is seen in a late-nineteenth-century dress.

This pair may be ancestors of Marilyn Willis. Holding the status of the handsomest unidentified couple the author has encountered, they present too fine an appearance to omit for the mere fact that we do not know their names.

The Cooke family includes Polly Cooke Willis (seated at left), grandmother of the lender, Marilyn Willis. Polly's mother (unidentified) is to her left, while her father, Thomas Cooke, is adjacent to Mildred, his daughter (with the large bow). A second daughter, Elsie, is seated at right, but the Cooke sons are unidentified.

Elizabeth Chandler La Bau Willis, mother of the lender Marilyn, was born in 1913 and lived most of her life in Fair Haven. After brief employment with the New York Life Insurance Company, she retired to a career as a homemaker. Seen here in the 1930s, Elizabeth Willis died in 1987.

Jacob Brown, a grandson of the Jacob who bought Browns Lane property in 1830, is seen at his 100th birthday party in 1993. His sister Mae is to his left. He was educated at the Fisk Street School, had a varied career, staying longest with his butler's position with Edgar Knapp in Rumson. Healthy through his tenth decade, he was regularly seen bicycling through the area, at times traveling some distance, to such destinations as Freehold Raceway or Monmouth Park. Jacob died in 1994. (Photograph by Robert B. Ender.)

Virginia Smith Paine (center) and Evelyn Bennett (right) are dressed for Halloween in 1930 with an unidentified companion at the Willow Street School playground. The Russell home on Willow Street is in the background. The dog is gazing intently at something, but not the photographer.

Mae Brown Johnson, a sister of Jacob, is seen in 1976 when she lived on Browns Lane but was reminiscing about her New York entertainment career. She sang in her Sunday school church choir and studied dance, music, and home economics at the Manassas, Virginia, Industrial School, leaving for New York City in the 1920s. Mae danced at some of the city's finest nightclubs, returning to Fair Haven in the 1930s to open a summer boarding house in the family residence.

Six of the fourteen children of Charles Doughty gather for the funeral of a seventh brother, Benjamin, in 1916 at McCarters Woods, about opposite the school on Willow Street. They are, from left, Nathan, William B. (grandfather of the lender, Richard F. Doughty), John, Robert, Charles, and Joseph.

This well-composed group is sitting on what appears to be a River Road lawn. One expects that the Chandlers are represented in this unidentified crowd.

Nathan J. Williams was born 1848. He was a carpenter and fence builder who erected the house at 21 Gillespie Avenue that is still in the family. He was a 32nd-degree Mason, and the N.J. Williams Lodge in Red Bank was named for him. Williams died in 1909.

Thomas Carlock, a building inspector, was a famed carver of birds, notably eagles. He is seen in 1982 with examples made for the Capitol in Washington.

Margaret Williams, nee Brown, born in 1850, married Nathan J. Williams. Their only child, Lillian, married a Cape May teacher, but the couple summered in Fair Haven. Biographical details are scant, but one old-timer recalls that Margaret "made delicious cakes." She died in 1918.

123

This may be the youthful Nettie Chandler in the 1890s.

Nettie Chandler was the only daughter of Christopher Doughty Chandler and the former Mary Elizabeth Greene (the couple had one son who died in childhood). She was born on July 1, 1879, in Fair Haven and married James La Bau. Her father photographed her on September 19, 1909.

This woman appears not to be pleased at being photographed, perhaps because she is showing more of a "winter suit of armor" than of herself. The outfit merits preservation, even in the absence of the wearer's name.

Fish hawks fascinated early photographers, who sought them on their high perches. Birders still seek them, and Sandy Hook is one of this species' contemporary homes. Here is a terrestrial bird, photographed on November 7, 1908, by Christopher Chandler, brought to you by the Historian of Fish Hawk Drive.

In 1904, Dr. Robert Dickson bought a little over 20 acres of Charles Parker property on Kemp Avenue from Charles McCue, who had held it briefly. Dickson and wife, Jennie, from New York, maintained Brookside Farm for the next fifteen years, selling the property to Orray Thurber in 1919. The image is from a 1909 postcard.

The author has seen many man-and-dog pictures in which the canines are more attentive than the humans. But look at these six who are all over the place! The horse wants to be in, but has to be satisfied with a distance shot. Presumably Dr. Dickson is at right, photographed in 1909.

Dr. Dickson raised prize-winning fowl, as are seen below. It is not clear if this stock is for show, breeding, or the table. Chandler photographed the birds in 1909.

Dr. Robert Dickson's Single Comb Rhode Island Reds won one of four first prizes and one of three second prizes at the Monmouth Poultry Club on February 27, 1909. More than one hundred poultrymen exhibited over fourteen hundred chickens, ducks, pheasants, turkeys, geese, and other fowl. One wonders how large the clean-up crew was.

Hap Handy was a vaudevillian. His act involved the manipulation of soap bubbles, obviously a routine that should be seen rather than described. Handy is seen in front of his house at 89 Willow Street (p. 37) with a pair of goats in the summer of 1911.

Gene Handy is using two goats to pull three friends for a ride in the summer of 1911. The author, pleased to have this fine goat cart example for his favorite ending, has a girl goat cart driver waiting for Volume II. So, keep those pictures coming! His address and phone number are on p. 8.